TABLE OF
contents

C000217309

INTRODUCTION

by Desmond Morris

For the Manwatcher, pubs are a gold mine. They are bursting with body language, awash with human encounters and rife with minor rituals. When you settle down in the corner of any pub, you find yourself attending an entertaining beer-opera more absorbing than any soap-opera.

In a strange way, pubs bring out the best in people. They turn couch-potatoes into bar-performers; convert the shy into the confident, the mumbling into the articulate and the solitary into the sociable.

Why should this be? What is the secret of the pub that gives it such an ageless popularity, able to withstand social upheavals that have seen the end of the local music hall and the local cinema?

The answer can be found by casting an enquiring eye on the customs of primitive tribes. Anthropologists have discovered that, almost everywhere they look, social drinking rituals are an essential part of the simple, non-industrial cultures.

In many cases there are small ceremonies to be observed. Drinks are shared and passed around, special vessels are employed, and songs are sung. Often, extra drinks are poured for the local deities, on the basis that, if they are any good as gods, they must enjoy a little nip, like the rest of us. Evidence of these libations is found time and time again, as archaeologists explore the world of our ancient ancestors. Clearly, we are dealing with a deep-seated pattern of human behaviour that is thousands of years old.

Wild bears have also been observed in a cheerfully inebriated condition after feasting on fermented fruits.

Indeed, there is nothing uniquely human about enjoying a drop of alcohol. In the wilds of Africa, elephants often get tipsy from drinking fermenting fruits. They stagger, ever so slightly, as they stride along, and flap their ears more than usual, feeling a trifle over-heated. An elephantine hangover, following nightmares about pink humans, hardly stands thinking about, but the next day they come back for more, gathering around the over-ripe fruit trees in noisily slurping groups.

Later, with the farming developments of the New Stone Age, cultivated grains could be used, and a whole technology sprang up.

Throughout its long history, alcohol was used as the lubricant for social bonding. Solitary drinking was for the sad and the sick. The rest of the world gathered in lively groups to pass the time of night with stories and songs, as the chemistry of the alcohol worked its magic.

This magic was twofold. First, it acted directly on the physiology of the drinkers, reducing their levels of anxiety. This helped to free them from the cares of the day, and from the social inhibitions which their fears and anxieties had created. They enjoyed the luxury of becoming more open and honest with each other - in vino veritas - and of relaxing momentarily from the stresses of their regular, workaday existence.

Second, the alcohol provided them with an on-going diversion to occupy them during their friendly coming-together. They were not drinking to quench their thirst - not after the first drink, anyway - nor, in most cases, to get hopelessly drunk. They were instead drinking as a way of enhancing the social time spent together. This is why so many ancient and tribal drinking sessions involved special rituals - from lighthearted competitions and status displays to the uttering of chants and incantations.

All these procedures helped to make the simple act of taking a drink more complicated and more prolonged. In this way, they helped to keep the group together in a friendly, playful, essentially non-serious mood and, in so doing, gave the lengthy sessions a socially therapeutic value. The drinkers may have suffered a little the next morning - even the ancient Greeks complained about hangovers - but all through the long evening they were benign and open and loved their fellow-men.

This is more than just a few people having fun. This is social binding of a very basic kind. It is so fundamental that one can observe its equivalent in our closest animal relatives, the great apes. Gorillas will spend long sessions, sitting quietly together

4

after a long foraging bout, grooming one another's fur. They appear to be cleaning one another, but this is not important, any more than quenching the thirst is important to human drinkers. They would do it even if their fur was immaculate. What is vital to them is that they should have some sort of friendly, shared activity that they can perform while they are close together, as a 'displacement activity' or diversion, to make the act of staying close to one another easier to carry out. Taking turns to groom one another's fur is their version of taking turns to buy one another a round in a modern pub. Reciprocity, mutual aid and social sharing are crucial parts of the ceremony, whether with friendly gorillas or with sociable human pubgoers.

This is nothing new. Back in ancient Babylon, the ruler Hammurabi decreed that the introduction of political debate into the 'beer-shops' - the pubs of those days - would be punishable by death. Although this helpfully served to keep the drinking atmosphere cheerful, it has to be admitted that the ruler's true motive was more likely to prevent his people discussing him when they were in an open, uninhibited frame of mind. Honesty and politics have always been uneasy bedfellows.

Given that there is so much more to pubs than the quenching of thirsts, what can we learn by a little judicious Pubwatching? We can find out, if we are objective enough, just how well the modern premises fulfil the ancient requirements of those who visit them.

If we observe carefully the actions of modern pubgoers, and relate them to the timeless social needs of our species, we may be able to detect where today's pubs are occasionally going wrong and where - much more frequently - they are going very right indeed. That is the aim of this Pubwatching research project.

To create the right atmosphere for friendly bonding to take place, pubs must have a special visual quality. They must look like pubs and like nothing else. With their external sign-boards and their internal decorations, they must stand apart from other kinds of buildings, proclaiming that here, things are different. Here, the dreary stressful parts of life are left outside. No solemnity permitted on these premises.

CHAPTER ONE

Pubs and people

Why do we go to pubs?

The pub is by far the most popular leisure venue in Britain. There are more than seventy thousand pubs in Britain, with over twenty-five million regular customers. Over three-quarters of the population go to pubs, and over a third are regular pub-goers, visiting a pub at least once a week.

So what gives the pub such a prominent place in our culture and society? What essential function does it serve?

All pubs serve drinks, and we might assume that this is the common denominator, the essential function of the pub. But if we look a bit closer, it is clear that the customers in our local pub are not just "here for the beer".

After all, if we just wanted to drink, we could all buy our beer, wine, spirits and soft drinks from supermarkets or off-licences and stay at home. It would certainly be cheaper. What instinct drives us to abandon our armchairs and televisions, put on our coats and venture out into the cold and rain to get to the pub instead?

The answer, of course, is sociability. We are social animals, we need to be with other people, and we need a friendly, sociable context in which to meet. During the research, we asked several hundred pubgoers the simple question "Why do you go to pubs?". Although a few did mention drinking, their answers also invariably included the words 'socialising', 'company' or 'meeting friends'.

We could, of course, invite friends to drink, eat and socialise in our own homes - and visit them in theirs. But in our society, this represents a far higher level of intimacy than meeting in a public place. We can happily meet people regularly in a

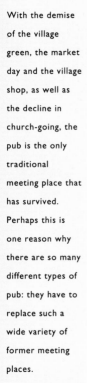

With the demise of the village green, the market day and the village shop, as well as the decline in church-going, the pub is the only traditional meeting place that has survived. Perhaps this is one reason why there are so many different types of pub: they have to replace such a wide variety of former meeting places.

6

'public house', whom we would never dream of inviting into our 'private house'. The term 'pub' is so widely used that we have perhaps forgotten its origins: it is short for 'public house', and never was an institution more aptly named.

'Public house' accurately describes the function of the pub in our society. A pub is a house, whose 'front room' is open to the public. In many ways, this front room (or rooms) may be like our own, designed for receiving and entertaining, with chairs and small tables, only on a larger scale and decorated in a more "extrovert" manner. The landlord or licensee is referred to as the 'host', as we would call anyone giving a party in their own home. This resemblance to home gives us a sense of safety and security. As one woman put it "It's so welcoming. It's a bit like being at home, isn't it? It's so cosy, so comforting."

At the same time, it is a public place. We have no responsibility for the other 'guests'. We do not have to worry about damage to the furniture, or clearing up afterwards. We may come and go as we please, drink or eat what we like, make new friends, or stick with our regular companions. We can be as outgoing or as reserved as we choose. The 'public' nature of the pub gives us a sense of freedom and excitement.

This also explains many of the contrasts between different types of pub. They can all be positioned on a scale in terms of the balance between freedom and security that they offer.

The 'circuit' pub or disco-bar, for example, would be at the 'high-freedom' end of the scale: there are very few home-like features in the decor, which deliberately sets out to create an atmosphere of excitement and energy, rather than comfort and relaxation. This is because the circuit pub caters for young people, who tend to have a much greater desire for freedom and novelty than for security and familiarity. The pub is their escape from the perhaps stifling security of home and family. The last thing they want is to be reminded of home. Even at this extreme, however, there is still an element of security - demonstrated by the large number of single females to be found here - but it is never oppressive. To keep up with young people's insatiable demand for novelty, circuit pubs are redecorated far more frequently than any other type.

The traditional 'village' or 'family' pub, catering mainly for an older age-group with different priorities, would lie at the opposite, 'high-security' end of the scale. There will be plenty of reminders of home in the decoration, a greater emphasis on comfort and cosiness, and, perhaps, an avuncular landlord who will chat about the weather and listen sympathetically to customers' problems. Again, even the 'high-security' pub will exhibit some freedom-oriented features. Colours on walls and carpets will be bolder and more intense than those we would use in the home, and the decoration in general will be more elaborate and 'larger than life' than our own living rooms. A pub which looked exactly like our own front room would certainly give a sense of security, but we would not bother to leave home to sit in it. We want a degree of excitement and stimulation, even in very 'homey' pubs.

Most other types of pub fall somewhere between these two extremes on the 'freedom-security' scale, some will lean slightly more towards freedom and excitement, others will tip the balance in favour of comfort, homeliness and safety. Pubgoers instinctively choose the balance which best meets their needs. And although these needs may change with age, or even with the time of day or the pub-goer's mood, there will always be a pub that fits.

What is a typical pub?

You make friends with some Americans while on holiday in Florida. The following year, they come to visit you, and ask to be shown a 'typical British pub'. Where would you take them?

You might decide to play it safe, and take your guests to the pub most likely to match their preconceived stereotype of a 'traditional' pub. This will probably be the thatched, 'olde worlde' type of pub they may have seen on calendars or in tourist guides.

Or you might decide to surprise them, to take them to a very basic town-centre 'boozer', or perhaps a trendy 'circuit' pub, or a council-estate community pub.

Whatever your choice, you will probably feel frustrated. This is because you know that no single pub can possibly give your visitors an accurate picture of pub life in Britain. The problem - for the visitor, not the native pub-goer - is that there is such a rich variety of different types and styles of pub. We may have to tell our guests the truth, that there is no such thing as a 'typical' pub.

But how do we educate our visitors? How would you explain the differences between the different types of pub they will encounter on their travels? What would you advise them to look out for? Some of the features which characterise particular types of pub are obvious, but others are far less easy to detect. And pubs do not come conveniently labelled.

Pubs are not always easy to categorise. We may use a number of different terms to describe the same type of pub. At the same time, the label 'traditional' is now applied to almost any pub which is not blatantly modern, and has thus become almost meaningless without further qualification. Despite these arbitrary and subjective definitions, we can still identify some of the more distinctive styles, and how to spot them.

The Serious-traditional pub

This is just one of the many types of 'traditional' pub, but it can easily be differentiated from what we might call the 'tourist-traditional' pub, and from other 'traditional' styles such as the 'stockbroker' or 'green-wellie' pub - if we know what to look for.

The most obvious difference is the attitude towards beer. All pubs serve the stuff, and many now offer a range of traditional cask-conditioned ales - known as Real Ales. But in the serious-traditional pub, greater importance is attached to the authenticity of the ales, and this concern for historical accuracy is reflected in other aspects of the pub.

Decor

'Traditional', but can be distinguished from other 'traditional' style pubs by a certain self-conscious minimalism. The message is clearly " We're here for the beer, not the trimmings".

There is nothing too chintzy, olde worlde or contrived. If there are horse-brasses, they will be real (like the ale), not mass-produced imitations. The same goes for any wood panelling or beams - as though anything fake might cast doubt on the 'reality' of the beer. Definitely no plastic, chrome, neon, bright colours or anything high-tech: these are associated with the despised 'keg' beers. Jukeboxes, games machines and even pool tables are treated with similar suspicion, although there may be a bar-billiards table.

Customers

Generally middle-class, and in the 25-50 age group. Mostly male, with some accompanying females. Very few lone females or all-female groups.

Serious-traditional pubs are often favoured by students, as well as social workers, teachers, university lecturers and other dedicated, non-profit-making professionals. The clientele may well also include members of CAMRA (the Campaign for Real Ale), who are drinking for a cause, as well as for the taste. A few amiable eccentrics, and the occasional train-spotter, are scattered among the ordinary folk who appreciate a good pint.

Service

Usually friendly, relaxed and unhurried. Polite, although the response to a request for a lager-and-lime ranges from the raised eyebrow to the disapproving stare.

Atmosphere

Sociable, sometimes hearty. The more isolated serious-traditional pub may feel a bit like a club. Many customers will probably be regulars, but even those who do not know each other share an appreciation of quality and authenticity.

If you don't know your Tanglefoot from your Ruddles, admit it and profess willingness to learn. You will not only be accepted, but should acquire any number of mentors who will be only too delighted to educate you.

The Circuit pub

Also known as 'Trendy' pubs 'Fun' pubs 'Venue' pubs or 'Disco-bars', circuit pubs are now to be found in many city centres. Within this broad category, however, there is a great variety of different styles. Some circuit pubs may be barely recognisable as pubs, as they share so many of the standard features of discotheques or night-clubs. Others may be

Whatever the chosen
style, which may
range from bright-
blue-and-chrome to
fire-engine-red-with-
brass to
'sophisticated' black
and grey, the circuit
pub will appear fresh,
clean and newly-
decorated. There will
be no comfortable
shabbiness, no
mismatched furniture
and no scratched,
wobbly tables. If
there were horse-
brasses, which is
most unlikely, they
would be six-foot-
high gimmicks, made
of pink papier-mache.

deceptively traditional from the outside. These clues help us to identify the true circuit pub.

Decor

Bright lights are an essential feature of the circuit pub. People are there to see and to be seen, to show off, not to huddle in private corners. If you enter a city-centre pub which appeared fairly ordinary and traditional from outside, and find it exceptionally brightly lit and sparkling indoors, you may well have stumbled on a circuit pub. If it has an open-plan design, with lots of mirrors and shiny surfaces, and perhaps a small dance floor, you know you are in a circuit pub.

There may also be raised areas in the most brightly-lit parts of the pub. These are known as 'posing platforms', and are there to 'display' the most confident and 'extrovert' of the circuit drinkers.

Customers

Invariably young: circuit pubs cater almost exclusively to the 18-25 age group. Circuit-pub customers come into town on Friday and Saturday nights, and spend the evening parading from pub to pub within a well-defined area, often staying only long enough for one drink in each venue. This custom is generally known as 'circuit drinking', although each town may have its own terminology. In Wakefield, for example, it is called 'Doing The Westgate Run' after the street in which the circuit pubs are located.

This is one of the few pub types where you are likely to see an equal number of males and females, often in large single-sex groups. All customers will be in their very best 'gear', and both males and females will clearly have taken a great deal of care over their appearance.

Service

Usually fast and cheerful, occasionally flamboyant. Circuit pubs will be very busy, particularly on Friday and Saturday nights, so the bar staff will have no time for leisurely chats. Like the customers, however, they are 'on display', and some may take a great deal of pride in their own speed and dexterity. A few will give virtuoso 'performances': pouring several pints at once, while shaking a cocktail in each hand, then whisking the glasses from under the taps in the nick of time and placing the drinks on the bar with a flourish.

Atmosphere

Bubbly, bright, noisy, crowded, exuberant. Everyone is there to show off. Groups of males and females will be eyeing each other with feigned indifference. They will exchange provocative insults and good-natured banter in the usual, time-honoured courting rituals.

In one village pub the only indication that children are welcome is a small, handwritten notice in the window which reads "Children are asked to ensure the good behaviour of their parents"

The Family pub

These are a fairly recent phenomenon, and a genuine 'response to popular demand' by the brewers and pub-operating companies. Market research (or the MD chatting with a few pubgoers) indicated that young parents who enjoy going to pubs were inhibited by the 'exclusion' of their children. Although pubs have always been legally allowed to welcome children accompanied by their parents, providing they used a room or defined area without an actual bar, in practice this usually meant sitting outside in the beer garden - not much fun in February!

The operating companies seized this obvious opportunity and 'created' the Family Pub.

This is a very wide category, ranging from the 'specialist' family steak-houses and pub/restaurants to the ordinary village pub which will serve half-portions if you ask for them. But if you're out with young children, and dying for a pint, you will be looking out for certain clues to tell you that you will be welcomed.

Decor

Some family pubs will be very easy to spot, even from a moving car full of frustrated kids. There will be large signs outside saying 'Family Pub' or 'Children Welcome' or promoting the latest 'Children's Menu'. You may even come across signs identifying the premises as a '*Traditional* Family Pub' or an '*Old Fashioned* Family Pub'. This is a something of a contradiction in terms, as children have, until very recently, never been actively welcomed in pubs. But historical accuracy is not important. The publican's aim is to please us, not to give us a history lesson. What such signs convey is the promise of a warm welcome and no plastic seats. This is exactly what we want: a real pub that welcomes children, not a MacDonald's with horse-brasses.

The pubs with large signs welcoming families or children tend to be those owned by breweries or major operating companies.
'Family' pubs run by independent publicans may be less easy to identify, although those with tables in the garden, particularly if they also offer hot meals, are usually worth trying.

Inside, most family pubs will be

decorated in a standard 'traditional' manner. Even those which specialise in catering for parents with young children may look deceptively like 'normal' pubs. If you go to pubs to get away from family and children, do not rely on swings and climbing frames to put you off, as these may be tucked away in a garden behind the pub. You may have to look for smaller clues - such as table mats in suspiciously bright, primary colours, or smiley faces on one of the menu blackboards - before deciding to make your escape.

Customers

Even in 'specialist' family pubs, those with young children will be restricted to a 'restaurant' or other specially designated areas. These pubs may also cater mainly for families at lunch time and in the early evening, with an entirely adult clientele after about 9 pm. Pubs which merely accept children, rather than encouraging them, will probably be completely child-free in the evenings. In pubs with a 'family' bias, however, you are more likely to see unaccompanied females - although not in equal proportion to single males, as in the circuit pub. There will also be a higher percentage of couples than in other pub categories. In the evening, most of the adult family-pub customers will be over 30, although younger parents will be seen at lunch time.

Service

Generally cheerful and attentive. In the big specialist pubs the staff will be well trained, polite and efficient. In the small village or country pub the service style will be more personal.

Atmosphere

Usually quiet, relaxed and friendly, although there may be some liveliness and bustle at lunch time. Background music will be unobtrusive, and you will rarely find any rowdiness or flamboyant behaviour. Customers are there to relax, to chat over a pint or two, or to enjoy a simple, inexpensive meal. The atmosphere of the smaller, village type of family pub will be more cosy and home-like, but even the larger, brighter 'specialist' variety will have something of that 'front-room' feel to it.

The Estate pub

This is perhaps the most interesting of the pub types, and, along with the 'town-centre corner boozer', probably the most genuinely traditional. These are the pubs which cater to a particular local population, rather than a 'customer type' desired by the publican, or identified through market research. A pub on a large council or housing estate attracts little if any passing trade, and cannot 'target' a particular section of the community. Even in a village, the publican can, to some extent, choose his customers. He can adjust his decor, menu, facilities and service style to attract either the 'green wellie' crowd or the local 'lads'. The estate pub has none of these modern freedoms. The customers are the local community, and the publican must take them as they come. Strictly speaking, then, an estate pub is any pub situated on a council or other housing estate. But they do share a number of other features, and dedicated pubwatchers could identify an estate pub even if they were taken to it blindfolded.

Decor

Estate pubs are usually big, sprawling places, with two or more large bars. Some will even have a separate pool or games room, and perhaps a function room upstairs. Unless the pub has been very recently refurbished, the decor will have a comfortable shabbiness about it. However clean and tidy, the place will have a 'lived-in' feel. It will have many home-like features, but will be more like your slightly scruffy 'family room' than your formal 'front room'.

The estate pub decor is often more genuinely home-like than the so-called 'traditional' pub - after all, how many of us have real log fires in our living rooms? In most ordinary homes, we are far more likely to find the worn carpets and well-used furniture of the estate pub.

Along with the home-like features, there will be reminders that you are in a public place, and that you are there to be entertained and enjoy yourself. You will see handmade posters advertising music nights, quiz nights, darts matches or charity events. There may also be the occasional 'Happy Birthday Joan' or 'Terry and Louise: Silver Wedding' and so on, indicating that the pub is very much the social centre of the local community.

Customers

Unless your visit takes place on a Karaoke night, music night or other crowd-pulling event, all of the customers will be local 'regulars'. The publican will know them all by name, or frequently by nickname. The estate pub is the focal point of the community. For the locals, it is their meeting place, and a 'home-from-home' in which to relax, or to show off, as their temperament dictates. You will find customers of all ages and in all combinations, from groups of 'unattached' young males and females, to middle-aged couples and singles, to old-age pensioners.

Many estates house large extended families, and you may well find that a number of the customers are related to each other. In one extreme example, an estate publican who attempted to 'bar' two feuding families for causing trouble in his pub soon found that he would have no customers at all, as almost the entire estate consisted of relatives of one or the other family.

Service

Friendly, but never ingratiating. These are not tourist pubs, and there will be no 'yes sir, certainly sir, ice-and-lemon sir' attempts to make you feel important. You are unlikely to find any impersonal customer-service-training-manual approaches here. The welcome will be genuine, the conversation unforced and easygoing. If you've just moved to the area, the publican will be your primary source of local information.

Atmosphere

The estate pub is very much a regulars' pub, and on an ordinary night it may feel a bit like a 'closed' community, with its own rites, rituals and unspoken codes of conduct. Much of the conversation and behaviour may initially be incomprehensible to outsiders. But an enquiry about a local event, or even a simple request for directions, can generate a lively exchange of views among your fellow customers. Always remember that the pub is their 'home', however, and treat it with respect.

The Student pub

Not only are student pubs instantly recognisable, but if you find yourself in one, you can be sure that you are no more than a mile from the university, poly or college from which the pub gets its trade. Unless their educational establishment is situated well outside the nearest town, students never move far from their 'home territory' in search of beer and amusement.

Decor

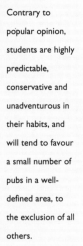

Contrary to popular opinion, students are highly predictable, conservative and unadventurous in their habits, and will tend to favour a small number of pubs in a well-defined area, to the exclusion of all others.

The 'dedicated' student pub will be immediately obvious: a cross between an ordinary pub and a student-union bar. Standard pub decorations, such as horse-brasses or framed old-fashioned drinks advertisements, will rub

shoulders with ill-printed posters promoting university or poly events and other newsheets or sources of vital information. There may even be framed photographs commemorating successful university sports teams, along with scarves, flags and other signs of tribal identification.The less blatantly student-oriented pubs will nonetheless contain one or two of these tell-tale elements.

In the majority of student pubs, furnishings will tend to be fairly robust and well-used, with no obvious attention to colour co-ordination or stylish trimmings. Although of roughly the same age as typical circuit-drinkers, students share none of their concern for sophisticated and well-designed surroundings.

Customers

Students. Although some student pubs may also cater to a 'business' clientele at lunch time and perhaps in the early evening, from 8-9pm onwards they are entirely dominated by students.

In some towns, university and polytechnic students will frequent the same pubs, while in others - usually those with the more established and venerable universities - there will be a rigid segregation. Where this is the case, the two student 'types' will be fairly easy to distinguish. Poly students look like normal people, and will all be dressed in exactly the same casually scruffy approximation of current fashion. University students tend to make more personal statements in their dress, and are consequently less immediately identifiable as a 'tribe'. In either case, you may well see almost equal numbers of males and females.

Service

Good-humoured, relaxed and tolerant. Bar staff will often be students themselves, and clever licensees employ the natural 'leaders' among the student population, knowing that they will attract a following.

Atmosphere

Noisy, cheerful and carefree - with an element of hysteria around exam-time. There will be a few 'couples', but students tend to go around in groups, and these may be as large as those found in circuit pubs. Many of the customers will know each other, and the atmosphere of a dedicated student pub will resemble that of the student-union bar. If you are over 30, you may look, and feel, somewhat out of place.

The Yuppie pub

The 'u' in the acronym 'yuppie' originally stood for 'urban', not 'upwardly mobile' as has been assumed. And there were pubs catering for 'young urban professionals' long before the activities of 'yuppies' began to interest the media in the early 1980s. Yuppie pubs are to be found in most city centres, in the 'smarter' areas of town. How do we recognise them?

Decor

Ranges from the classy wine-bar to the more traditional up-market pub. Considerable attention is paid to attractive design, although 'themes' will be much less obvious than in the circuit pub. Yuppie pubgoers are equally demanding, but tend to expect a more subtle, 'grown-up' style than circuit drinkers. Gimmicks and unusual decorations must be witty, tasteful, relatively unobtrusive and preferably expensive. You will find none of the ubiquitous 'job-lot Victoriana' here. You may well see blackboards advertising a variety of wines and champagnes, or scrambled eggs with smoked salmon served in miniature frying pans. The decor in some yuppie pubs may appear to have few home-like features, but then many yuppie homes give the same impression.

Customers

'Young urban professionals' comprises a considerably wider range of people and professions than the stereotyped City-dealers-with-Porsches. Most customers will be in the 24-35 age-group, and a variety of professions will be represented, generally including a large proportion of media-related occupations such as advertising, PR, television, publishing and so on.

Small groups and couples will predominate, with the occasional larger gathering celebrating a promotion, birthday or important contract. The pub will be particularly busy at lunch time and in the early evening.

Service

Very polite, courteous, unobtrusive and efficient. Customers do not expect long, cosy chats with the licensee or bar staff, but they do expect them to know their wine list, and to be familiar with all the latest brands of designer lager.

Atmosphere

Bright and sparkling - with a touch of self-consciousness in the manner and behaviour of the clientele. They are there to 'see and be seen' just as much as their counterparts in the circuit pubs, but their displays are neither so obvious nor so honest as those of the circuit drinkers.

Variety

These are just a few of the many different types and styles of pub from which we may choose. Other distinctive types would include the 'stockbroker' pub - similar to the yuppie pub but with an older clientele, and fewer single females. 'Stockbroker' pubs are to be found both in town centres and in well-heeled suburban areas.

The 'green wellie' pub is the country version of the yuppie and stockbroker pubs, where the same customers shed their city finery in favour of chunky jumpers, Barbour jackets and the inevitable green wellingtons.

While this simplified categorising provides pubwatchers with an endless source of amusement, it cannot begin to describe the variety and complexity of pub life. It is clear that many pubs do not fit easily into such pre-determined pigeon-holes.

Although some pubs may cater to a particular type of clientele, most pubs have a wide cross-section of customers in terms of age, social class and occupation. In fact, pubs may rightly be seen as the greatest 'leveller', the true 'classless society' where builders' labourers are to be found playing pool with professors, and market-stall vendors discuss the recession with their counterparts on the stock exchange.

A pub may also 'change categories' on weekends, or even from daytime to evening. Many attract a 'business' trade at lunch time, and perhaps from 5.30 to around 7.30 in the evening, but are entirely dominated by students or other young people from 7.30 until closing time. An ordinary town pub may become a circuit pub almost 'by default' through being located 'on the circuit' - on the route from one circuit venue to another.

Even within a particular category, no two pubs are alike: each pub has its own personality, its own unique atmosphere.

So how do we choose a pub?

In the course of our research, we asked several hundred people the same question: "What sort of pub do you prefer?". Their answers were as varied as the pubs they frequented. It is not just that some people want a quiet, cosy place where they can have a chat with their friends, while others seek a more lively, exciting atmosphere.

All pubgoers have their individual preferences, and often highly specific requirements. We all seem to know, instinctively, as soon as we come through the door, whether or not it is 'our sort of pub'. The requirements of the pubgoers we interviewed were often so precise that we wondered how such choosy people ever found the pub they wanted.

One young man, for example, was only interested in what he called "Eighties" pubs, and then only the ones that played chart music from the early eighties - no other period would do. Another would only consider "Heavy Metal" pubs, and then only if they also had pool tables and his favourite brand of lager. A very stylish young woman preferred "Showbar" pubs with a 'sixties' theme, while another gave her custom exclusively to American-style cafe-bars with pin-ball machines.

Some pubgoers want particular types of live entertainment (comedians, chart music, folk music, jazz bands, bluegrass bands, pub theatre - the list is endless). Others prefer to take a more active part in the proceedings, insisting on the most up-to-date Laser-Karaoke systems, or the latest video games.

Even among 'traditionalists', there is an enormous variety of different tastes to be catered for. Many young parents are enthusiastic about the 'family' pub, and will seek out those with the most attractive gardens, the greatest variety of swings and climbing frames or the best children's menus. Other traditionalists are more concerned about the authenticity of the decor and the quality of the cask-conditioned ale. They want a pub where the landlord or bar staff will happily engage in lengthy debates about the qualities and relative merits of their favourite beers.

The less serious may prefer a more 'chocolate-box', villagey type of traditionalism, with roses around the door, and log fires and home-made soup in the winter. There are even those 'traditionalists' who yearn for a return to the very basic, spit-and-sawdust 'boozer'. One man described his ideal pub as "dirty, smoky and gritty!"

Despite their often idiosyncratic desires, none of the pubgoers we interviewed had experienced any difficulty in finding pubs to meet their requirements. There are even traditional 'country' pubs in city centres, and trendy 'theme' pubs in small market towns. It seems as though you only have to decide on the environment, atmosphere, decor and type of service and entertainment that you want, and there will be a choice of pubs to suit you.

We also choose different types of pub for different occasions, at different times of day or even to suit different moods. With the enormous variety of styles to choose from, we take it for granted that all our whims, desires and passing fancies will be catered for. We know that there will always be a pub that meets our needs.

There may also be social or 'diplomatic' reasons for selecting different types of pub, and 54% of respondents said that their choice of pub would depend on whom they were going out with. A number of young men told us that they

In a recent survey, 57% of respondents said that they chose different pubs for different occasions. Many pubgoers, for example, will choose a quiet pub with good food at lunch time, even though the evening will find them dressed to kill in a trendy, noisy circuit pub.

would choose a "posh" or "trendy" place if they were going out with a girl, but for a night out with the lads, the priorities would be pool tables and a friendly atmosphere. Older males, again, would go to "upmarket" pubs with their wives, but tend to prefer a more basic boozer for a game of darts with their mates. Of course, many pubs have both 'lounge' and 'public' bars for precisely this reason.

Groups of friends will often meet up at the beginning of the evening in a quiet pub, and then move on to somewhere more lively - perhaps a Karaoke night, or a pub with live entertainment or a dance floor. As one young woman explained: "At the start of the evening, you want to catch up on each other's news, have a bit of a chat about whatever is going on, so you want to be somewhere quiet, where you can have a conversation. Later on, you want to have some fun, show off a bit, be in a crowd, you know, a bit of excitement - then you don't care if you have to shout to be heard!"

For some, the decision is more spontaneous, based purely on their mood on a particular night. Many pubgoers told us "It just depends on how I feel, what sort of atmosphere I want, what sort of people I want to be with."

Other factors, such as the type of amusements, games or entertainment on offer, will often influence our decisions. We may go to one pub because we are on their darts team, another when we want to listen to a good jazz band and a third to dance or play pin-ball.

While some people enjoy trying out new places, and will go to any pub that a friend or their local newspaper recommends "just to see what it's like", over 50% of pubgoers are 'regulars' in a particular local pub. Even if we don't have a 'local', many of us remain loyal to a few familiar pubs - although we will still make choices between them at different times of day, or for different occasions, purposes or moods.

For an observer of human behaviour, pubs are fascinating places. Pub behaviour is governed by a complex set of unspoken rules. From the elaborate procedure of getting served at the bar, through the intricate rituals of round-buying and conversation, to the reluctant departure at closing time, almost every interaction follows an unwritten code.

CHAPTER TWO

Whose round is it anyway?

We may not be aware that we are following these rules, but we soon notice, and often take great offence, when they are broken. The uninitiated tourist who taps a coin insistently on the bar counter and calls out "service" when he wants a beer will be the object of, at least, disapproving stares. He has failed to learn the tacitly accepted method of attracting the attention of bar staff.

Getting served

This is a complicated and subtle game, the object of which is to catch the barman's eye. This must be done without resorting to anything so direct, straightforward and effective as calling out, or even speaking at all.

Even when you have secured your position, you cannot relax and wait. You must shuffle and shift about like a racehorse at the starting gate, your gaze firmly fixed on the barman. If you look away for a split second, you may miss your chance to catch his eye.

You start by trying to identify the best position at the bar counter. If the pub is very busy, the favoured spot is usually directly opposite the till, as the bar staff must return there after each sale, giving you more opportunities to make eye contact.

Leaning your elbow on the bar with money in your raised hand is allowed, but raising your whole arm and waving the notes about is frowned upon.

Facial expressions must be anxious and expectant. If you look too calm and relaxed, the bar staff may assume that you are already being served.

All of these moves are played in silence. Coughing and muttering under your breath may be acceptable, but only after you have been ignored for some time. Even when you finally catch the barman's eye, he will rarely speak. A raised finger, with either a smile or a nod and a quick lift of the eyebrows, tells you that he has seen you waiting, and will serve you next. If you miss this gesture, or fail to respond with a nod and a smile, you may have missed your turn.

In most pubs, of course, you do not have to wait very long for this acknowledgement. Even when the bar is busy, you will soon receive a quick nod of recognition to put you out of your agony.

Most of us perform this tortuous pantomime automatically, without thinking - and certainly without questioning its effectiveness. Given the handicaps imposed by the unwritten 'rules of the game' - no speaking, no waving, constant alertness to tiny signals and so on - the uninitiated may be forgiven for wondering how anyone ever manages to buy a drink!

In fact, although many foreigners find it baffling, this procedure is remarkably efficient - a model of effective non-verbal communication. Everyone does get served, usually in the right order. This is because good bar staff are acute observers of body-language, and can pick up the most subtle cues and signals. There is simply no need to shout and wave at them. Your posture and expression tell them that you are waiting to be served; their small gestures of acknowledgement let you know that you are next.

Round-buying

Of course, you may not just be buying a drink for yourself. Even if you are only accompanied by one other person, you will be participating in the ancient tribal ritual of 'round-buying'.

The basic principle of round-buying is simple: in a group of two or more individuals, one will purchase a 'round' of drinks for the whole group. This is not done as an act of pure altruism. Gifts, as many anthropologists and psychologists have observed, are very rarely 'free'. There is always the expectation of a return, and reciprocal gift-giving is an important part of any social bonding. In round-buying, the expectation is that the other members of the group will each, in turn, buy a round of drinks. When each individual has bought a round, the process begins again.

Sit in any pub, listening to the conversations around you, and you will not have to wait long before you hear the traditional cries: "It's your round!", "It's my round, what are you having?", "Get the beers in, then.", "It's not my bloody round, I got the last one!", "What's yours?", "Whose round is it anyway?" and so on.

You may also overhear a few derogatory comments on individuals who avoid playing their full part in the ritual. Reputations are at stake, and those who bend the rules and shirk their responsibilities are soon exposed, labelled as tight-fisted, skinflints, free-loaders and downright mean.

Once established, a reputation for being tight-fisted tends to stick. Even a single omission can sometimes lead to weeks of 'jokingly' hostile remarks and reminders. Stung by these comments, and determined to restore their reputations, some individuals may over-compensate, buying more than their fair share, or always being the first to leap up with "It's my round".

The rare perpetual offender, impervious to all jokes, blandishments and reminders of his obligations, will soon find himself shunned by the rest of the group, and may well be doomed to drink alone, or move to another pub where his habits are not known.

To the uninitiated, there may appear to be very little equality or justice in the round-buying system. In one evening, for example, you may observe the same person buying two rounds, while other members of the group have only bought one. This usually happens when closing time interrupts the process. If "time, ladies and gentlemen" happens to strike in the middle of the ritual, then, inevitably, some members of the group will get off lightly, while others will not have received their full entitlement under the scheme.

There is, however, an element of trust in the round-buying system. The unspoken expectation is that at the next drinking session, the person whose turn it was to purchase drinks at the 'interrupted' session will buy the first round.

The trust between round-buyers must be fairly strong, as circumstances usually prevent the system from working out neatly and evenly. It is unlikely, for example, that the same group of people will be drinking together at every session, and most participants in the ritual are prepared to 'write off' any losses they may incur.

There are, of course, exceptions, qualifications and modifications to the rules of round-buying, but these are recognised as such, and generally remain within the basic principles of the ritual. There are situations where the standard round-buying system is simply impracticable: where, for example, the group of participants is so large that the cost of a 'round' would be prohibitive. In this event, the large group will often 'split' into smaller units, with individuals buying rounds according to the usual rules. Alternatively, the members of a large group may agree from the outset to purchase their own drinks. This is most often seen among students and others on low incomes.

Another variation of round-buying is the 'kitty' system, where each member of the group puts the same amount of money into a pool at the beginning of the evening. The 'kitty' method follows the same basic principle as more traditional round-buying, in that each individual is effectively buying drinks for the rest.

In the 'kitty' system, one member of the group will usually take responsibility for its administration. When the funds run out, the group will make a collective decision about putting in further amounts. If at the end of the session there is still money left in the 'kitty', it may be divided up equally among the group. By this time, however, a spirit of generosity may prevail, and you will hear "Oh, stick the rest in the charity box" or "You and the staff have a drink on us".

As with traditional round-buying, conflicts over the kitty system are invariably caused by those who feel that they are 'out of pocket', either because they are not drinking as much as the rest of the group, or because their drinks are less expensive. These are the same people who always want everything itemised on a restaurant bill, so that they only pay for exactly what they have eaten. In most cases, cries of "Don't be such a tight-arse" from their companions have the desired effect, but an occasional stubborn soul will end up drinking on his own.

Conversation

Eavesdropping on conversations in pubs can be highly entertaining. You will find out more about life in Britain by sitting in a pub and listening to what is said than by any other form of research. The British are generally quite reserved, and people rarely exchange confidences or discuss their concerns loudly enough to be heard in public places. The pub is the only exception.

So what do we talk about in pubs? In the late 1930s, a Mass Observation study identified the main topics of pub conversation

Speaking in 'code', which only the landlord and pub regulars can understand, is an important part of social bonding in pubs.

A 'private language' emphasises the strong links between members of the group. It helps to define them as a social unit, and to differentiate them from other groups. Children will often invent 'secret' languages for this reason, and the private 'codes' used by couples, or within families, serve the same function.

as: sport, betting, work, people, drinking, politics and dirt (by which they meant sex). As this covers pretty much everything, it is hardly surprising that not very much has changed.

It is not so much the subjects that make listening to pub-talk so fascinating, but the way people talk, the language that they use, the rules and rituals involved.

Coded conversation

Some overheard pub-talk may be difficult to decipher, particularly in 'local' pubs, where almost all the customers are 'regulars' and everyone knows each other. In such places, the conversation may appear to be in some sort of code, as no stranger could possibly understand it. Here is an example from our research, transcribed exactly as heard:

Customer 1: Where's Southampton then?

Landlord: Who?

Customer 2: Nobby.

Landlord: Oh, fatty? Dunno, tone.

Customer 1: Have the fixtures come out yet?

Landlord: No.

Customer 1: Hope we got a by.

Landlord: We'll probably end up at the feathers again.

Customer 1: Or the bloody grapes!
De-coded, this conversation turns out to be about people and

sport. Customer 1 is enquiring as to the whereabouts of a friend, who goes by the various nicknames of 'Southampton', 'Nobby' and 'Fatty'. The Landlord replies that he doesn't know, addressing Customer 1 by his own nickname 'Tone' (presumably short for Tony or Anthony).

Customer 1 then asks the Landlord if he has received the fixtures list that shows which pub darts teams will be playing against each other in the local league, and where the matches will take place. The Landlord replies that he has not.

Customer 1 then expresses his hope for a 'bye', which is a fortuitous 'exemption' from one stage, or 'round' of a series of matches, usually due to an uneven number of teams taking part. This would allow his team to proceed directly to the next round without having to win a match.

The Landlord then predicts that his pub's darts team will play an away match against the team of The Feathers, another local pub, while Customer 1 believes that it will be against The Grapes, a pub which he either dislikes, or which has a better team.

It can be difficult to join in such conversations. A friendly stranger, for example, might have misunderstood Customer 1's first enquiry and helpfully pointed out that Southampton is in Hampshire! But if you stay quiet and listen for a few evenings, you will soon begin to decipher the code.

Ritual conversations

You will also notice the underlying similarity of many pub conversations. Although the topics and settings may be very different, the tone will be the same, and certain conversations will follow a set pattern. We have already mentioned the almost choreographed "Whose round is it?" conversation, but there are many other ritual exchanges to listen for.

'Mine's better than yours'

Those familiar with standard pub-talk will instantly recognise the 'Mine's better than yours' conversation. This a ritual of one-upmanship which you may overhear in any type of pub, on any subject.

In a Lambourn pub, populated almost entirely by the stable lads who look after the racehorses trained in the village, the "Mine's better than yours" ritual will sound like this: "Mine'll beat yours easy on Saturday." "Rubbish, yours couldn't win if it started now. Old Starry's going to show yours the way home and that's a fact." "Bullshit, Starry's got a bad case of the slows and you know it." "Yeah, well the guv'nor says he'll walk it." "What does he bloody know? Stupid bugger couldn't train ivy up a wall." "Crap...." and so on.

In a pub dominated by cricket supporters, the conversation will be about the relative merits of rival teams. In a 'stockbroker' or 'yuppie' pub, it may concern the alleged superiority of the BMW over the Mercedes. Among rival football fans, 'Mine's better than yours' has become formalised to the extent that it is no longer a conversation at all, but a ritual chanting of set phrases and songs.

Whether we are talking about racehorses, football, cars, cricket or beer, the pattern of the conversation will be identical. This is because the "Mine's better than yours" ritual follows a formula, a set of unspoken but tacitly accepted rules.

'Mine's better than yours' always starts with a pronouncement or assertion which must be countered if the other person is to save face. It will always be countered, even if the target of the remark secretly agrees, or could not rationally disagree. The initiator expects this, and would be most disappointed if his target did not respond with a vehement defence and counter attack.

One could hardly even imagine a pub conversation where "Mine'll beat yours on Saturday" or "Don't know why you bother with that German thing, when you could have a Rover" elicited the response "Yes, I'm sure you're right". It would be unthinkable, an unprecedented violation of the rules. Attack must be followed by defence and counter-attack, which must in turn be countered.

As the ritual progresses, you will hear far more attack than defence, and the insults will become more and more elaborate. The exchange, however heated, will nonetheless seem fairly good-humoured, and the participants will continue to buy each other drinks. In fact, one of the most common ways of terminating the dispute is to finish a remark with "And anyway, it's your round" or "Get the beers in, then".

'Mine's better than yours' is an exclusively male pastime. Accompanying females may occasionally spoil the ritual exchange of insults by misunderstanding the rules and attempting to inject an element of reason. They also tend to become bored with the predictability of the formula long before their male companions have tired of the game. They may do something outrageous, such as asking the participants if they could not simply agree to disagree. Such interjections are usually ignored.

What these exasperated females fail to grasp is that there can be no rational resolution of such arguments. This is because they are no more genuine arguments than the chanting of rival football supporters. Football fans do not expect their chants to persuade their opponents to agree with them. And however spontaneous and inventive they may appear, "Mine's better than

There is no way to win the 'Mine's better than yours' game. No-one ever capitulates, or recognises the other's point of view. The participants simply get tired, or bored, and change the subject, perhaps shaking their heads in pity at their opponent's stupidity. They remain the best of mates.

yours" conversations are simply a less evolved form of ritual chanting.

'Don't fancy yours much'

Another 'formula' conversation you will almost certainly overhear is the 'Don't fancy yours much' exchange. Again, this is an exclusively male ritual, involving set phrases and expressions.

The set phrases used in this ritual are a sort of code, but not very difficult to interpret. The classic "Don't fancy yours much" is a standard comment on any pair of females, one of whom is considered less attractive than the other. As well as showing that he can tell the difference, the speaker is laying claim to the more attractive of the pair, by designating the less desirable one as 'yours'. In fact, the phrase is often used to comment on any female considered to be unattractive, whether or not she is accompanied by a more fanciable alternative. The fact that none of the objects of these remarks would be likely to give the commentators a second glance is immaterial.

"Not many of those to the pound" refers to the size of the observed female's breasts - suggesting that they are larger than average. It is an approving comment, often accompanied by a gesture indicating the weighing of heavy objects in the hands. "I would!" is a more general statement of approval, which requires no interpretation. "Definitely a ten-pinter" is a derogatory comment, the implication being that one would have to be extremely drunk even to contemplate sexual relations with the female in question.

Those who indulge most frequently in this ritual would probably become tongue-tied and embarrassed in the unlikely event of an actual

'Don't fancy yours much' is a form of the time-honoured and universal male pastime of commenting on the attributes of passing females. It is practised in pubs by males of all ages and social classes. If you overhear remarks such as "Not many of those to the pound" , "I would" or " Definitely a ten-pinter" you know that the speakers are engaged in the "Don't fancy yours much" ritual.

encounter with any of the targeted females. But that is not the point. 'Don't fancy yours much' is simply a ritual display of masculinity, performed entirely for the benefit of male companions. By reciting the standard lines, participants affirm their status as macho, active heterosexuals.

By tacit agreement, the assumption that they are in a position to pick and choose among the observed females is never questioned. The ritual thus allows participants to maintain the illusion that they are powerful and manly. Conspiring to promote this collective delusion also reinforces the social bonds between the participants.

Last orders and closing time

The cry 'last orders' has a strange psychological effect on us pubgoers. Even if we don't really want another drink, it draws us back to the bar. The publican calls out, or rings a bell, or flashes the lights, and like Pavlov's dogs, we suddenly feel thirsty.

As one landlady put it: "They can be drinking and chatting perfectly normally, but when you call 'last orders', something comes over them. They're like wild animals. They rush up to the bar, and they're pushing and they're shoving: it's like they're never going to get another drink in their lives."

Ironically, after our mad rush to buy the last pint, we then take an inordinate amount of time to drink it. After 'time' has been called, we drink even more slowly. Given twenty minutes 'drinking-up time', we make sure that the last drink takes at least that long - even though we've been quaffing twice the amount in half the time throughout the evening.

Like children who have been told it is bedtime, we linger and dawdle and find any excuse to stay up longer. "But I haven't *finished*," we whine, pointing to the half-centimetre of beer left in our glass. We huddle in corners, hoping that we won't be noticed. Although we know that we will have to leave, we won't go of our own accord, but have to be reminded every five minutes. Like a weary parent, the publican sighs and repeats "Come on, now. Let's have your glasses, please" until finally, grudgingly, we obey.

CHAPTER 3

The guv' nor

Many people's retirement fantasies involve 'buying a little pub in the country'. We see the landlord of our local chatting genially with friendly regulars, while pulling a few pints, and we think what a pleasant life it must be. We like going to the pub, and we imagine that having our own pub would be even better. We see the respect the publican commands, his standing in the community. We watch people buying him drinks, laughing at his jokes and asking his opinion. We notice that he always seems relaxed and cheerful, that he always has time for a chat, and we envy him this easygoing existence.

But what is it really like? How much do we really know about the view from the other side of the bar? What is being a publican all about?

There is, of course, the side we never see. The cellar work, the shifting of heavy boxes and crates, dealing with suppliers, doing the accounts, seeing to repairs, stock-taking, cleaning the toilets and training the staff. Everything that goes on behind the scenes, before the pub opens its doors, and after we have all gone home.

But even the side of the job that we do see is more complex and difficult than we imagine. It may look easy, but making it look easy is part of the job, part of what it takes to be a good publican. If we look more closely at the many roles of the landlord, we may wonder how any one person can possibly do the job.

The psychologist

Good publicans (and good bar staff) are probably the best students of human behaviour you will ever come across. They know more about body language that those of us who have spent years writing books on it. Good publicans are able to assess the mood of their customers at a glance, picking up subtle clues in our posture, gestures, facial expressions and tone of voice. Without asking, they can judge who would appreciate a friendly chat and who wants to be left alone. They can detect the signs of discord between a couple before the pair themselves are aware of any lack of harmony. They can tell if a customer has had a bad day or a good day, just from the way he enters the pub and walks to the bar. They can spot mutual attraction or unrequited love at twenty paces. They know what we are feeling, and can predict our behaviour.

More importantly, they know how to use this information - how to apply their knowledge. They know how to make us feel welcome, and they can anticipate our needs. They can judge when it is appropriate to laugh and tell jokes, and when we need someone just to listen to our problems and nod sympathetically. They will give advice or keep their thoughts to themselves as necessary. They will choose exactly the right moment to intervene in an argument, and know how to defuse any tensions between customers.

Ironically, the one thing they are not always aware of is their own expertise as psychologists. When you ask them how they assess mood and atmosphere, they will often look puzzled, and reply that it is obvious, or that it's just an instinct, or that you learn from experience. In a way, this is true. We all have a natural sensitivity to the atmosphere around us. If there are underlying tensions, we may feel uncomfortable, even if we don't know why. The difference is that good publicans have developed and fine-tuned this natural ability. They have to be able to read the signals, and know how to respond. Being better at this than most psychologists is nothing extraordinary: to them, it is simply part of the job.

The actor

Although the guv'nor is the star of the show, the centre of attention, not all of the roles have dignity. The publican is often required to play the stooge, the clown or the fall guy. As one landlord put it "You have to make a fool of yourself sometimes. They all love to have a laugh at the gaffer".

From the moment the doors open, the publican and the bar staff are 'on stage'. Their personal problems or worries must be forgotten, and they must become the characters their customers want to see.

Many of the publicans we interviewed during the research talked about the acting involved in running a pub. "You have to be whatever the customers want you to be," said one landlord "it's show-business, that's really the business were in."

Unlike the professional actor, however, the publican does not have the luxury of playing one part all evening. The publican may have to be a joker one minute, and an understanding auntie or parish priest the next. Nor are publicans allowed to play their parts and say their lines without interruption. They must constantly adapt their 'performance' to the mood and wishes of their audience.

Good publicans tend to be good talkers, and good entertainers. They have what the Irish call 'the gift of the gab'. They know that they are 'on show' and they are always ready with a joke, an anecdote or a bit of light-hearted banter. They never go on too long, though, and they never hog the limelight.

The community leader

The publican is often the 'cornerstone' of the local community. People come to him for advice. They expect him to act as arbitrator in their disputes, and to help solve their problems at work or at home.

The problems that publicans are expected to solve can be of a very serious and personal nature. One landlord told us "Someone's marriage was breaking up, and I managed to bring them back together by talking to them both. Someone's son was

The publican has, in
many communities,
taken over the role
and status of the
parish priest. He or
she also often acts
as a news service,
the main source of
local information,
as an informal
citizens advice
bureau, as a bank
and as a counsellor
or social worker.

not playing the game with his father, and his father was getting angry with him, so I had to solve that. I'm not a clever person. I haven't got any qualifications. But I can talk to people and understand them, and they look to me for advice."

One cannot imagine the owner or manager of any other local business being given such responsibility. Those who see running a pub as 'the same as any other retail business' had better think again. The manager of your local branch of Dolcis or Tesco would never be asked to resolve an argument or sort out a family problem. The manager of your 'local branch' of Whitbread or Bass will take it in his stride.

Publicans will also be expected to give their considered opinion on all local issues, from the plans to build a bypass to the fund-raising problems at the primary school. The publican is likely to know more about the private and public lives of the people in his area than anyone else. And he is usually a good judge of what to tell and what to keep quiet about.

Of course, the respect and status that publicans enjoy does not come automatically with the licence to sell drinks. It has to be earned. The publican gains the trust and confidence of the community through a careful balancing of friendly involvement with professional detachment. He or she must acquire a reputation for being fair, as well as firm and decisive. The good publican gains respect by treating all customers equally, with no favourites or cliques.

The policeman

Respect, of course, is not a luxury. If he cannot gain the trust and respect of his customers, the publican will soon be in trouble. This is because the publican also has to act as a policeman. He or she must enforce the law, and control the behaviour of customers, but without the automatic authority of the policeman's uniform.

Publicans must not serve people who have had a few too many. They are responsible for ensuring that no-one under eighteen can be served alcohol in their pubs. They have to prevent disorder, and remove people from the premises who are drunk, disorderly, or likely to annoy the other customers. They also have to enforce the licensing hours, getting everyone out of the pub by 11.20 at night.

These obligations can put publicans in a very difficult position. For a start, we do not normally expect civilians to enforce the law and restrict other people's actions in this way. It is even more difficult when you must control and restrict the behaviour of people who see you as a friend. Publicans do not wear a uniform or a badge. Any authority they have over their customers comes from their own treatment of those customers, from the personal respect and trust that they have worked very hard to gain.

These are only a few of the social roles of the average guv'nor. They also organise most of the local charity events, special functions and celebrations, musical evenings, sports, entertainment and games.

It is certainly not the easy life we imagine in our 'retirement' fantasies. You have to be a psychologist, an entertainer, a social worker, a surrogate parent, a police officer, a judge, a lawyer, a fund-raiser and a local news service - as well as trying to run a profitable business! It is not surprising that publicans have very little time to themselves.

So why do they do it? What are the rewards? One publican summed up the feelings of many when he told us "Your pub's a

Publicans devote on average 16 hours per month of their own time to work in local community organisations. Over a third give more than 20 hours per month to such groups.

way of life. It's your work and it's your social life rolled into one. Your customers become your friends. You get involved with them. You know about their families, when they have a baby, when they change their job, when they lose their job. The good and the bad, you hear it all."

The many social roles of the publican must each bring their own rewards. There is the counsellor's or social worker's feeling of fulfilment when a personal problem is resolved. There is the psychologist's delight in accurately assessing a situation, or predicting someone's behaviour. There is the arbitrator's pleasure in the resolution of a dispute, and the journalist's in being the first to know the latest news. There is, of course, the entertainer's sense of achievement when the audience laughs. Above all, there is the satisfaction of being at the centre of a community, becoming friends with your customers, and seeing their enjoyment of the environment and atmosphere that you have created.

CHAPTER 4

Play it again

Music is more than a pleasurable aesthetic experience. The tears of Olympic winners when their national anthem is played have nothing to do with any intrinsic qualities of the music: the athletes are moved by the feelings of national pride and belonging which are associated with the tune. Every culture, sub-culture and individual tribe has its own 'ritual music', its own distinctive 'anthems'.

If we are told that someone is a folk-music aficionado, or a disco fan, we will immediately make a number of other assumptions about that person's lifestyle - their style of dress, their politics, their home, where they go on holiday and so on. We are able to make these Sherlock Holmes deductions, not because we are brilliant detectives, but because their musical 'affiliation' tells us which tribe they belong to.

What kind of music do you like? Whatever your choice, there will be a pub where you can hear your tribal 'anthems', take part in the associated rites and rituals, and feel that you belong.

There has always been music in pubs, of course, but there is now more variety than ever before. In the course of our research, we found pubs which offered Folk music, Blues bands, Jazz bands, Sing-a-longs, Rock bands, Heavy metal music, Classical piano or guitar, Bluegrass bands, Disco music, Fifties music, Sixties music, Seventies music, Eighties music, current Chart Hits, 'Rave' music, Country and Western bands, Middle-of-the-road music, Bob Dylan nights, Jimi Hendrix nights, Soul music, Irish ballads, Scottish reels - even 'Abba revival nights' and Jiving lessons.

Many pubs now specialise in a

Our choice of music is as much a statement about ourselves as the clothes we wear or the way we decorate our homes. Our musical preference signals our membership of a particular 'tribe', a distinct social group with shared tastes, values and lifestyle.

particular kind of music, and some may become the 'official' local venue for that genre - the focal point for a particular 'music tribe'. There are 'specialist' jazz pubs, country-and-western pubs, rock pubs and so on. These venues will often have a club-like feel to them, as many of the customers will be regulars, devotees of the type of music that the pub provides, members of the same tribe. The music, to them, is an integral part of a 'bonding' ritual, a confirmation of their shared tastes, values and way of life. This tribal solidarity will be evident in their conversation and behaviour, much of which will be incomprehensible to outsiders.

In addition to the 'specialist' pubs, there are many which will have a different type of live music every week. Each band or type of music will have its own followers, although some of the pub's regular customers will turn up faithfully at every 'music night'. Their 'membership' of the pub is stronger than their affiliation to a particular music tribe.

Why is live music in pubs so popular?

Pub landlords and managers try to provide what their customers want. And they are very much aware of the attraction of live music. They know that the takings of a normally 'quiet' Wednesday night can be substantially increased by the presence of a live band. People will attend pub 'music nights' who never go to concerts, or listen to live music in any other context. We will go to our local pub to hear a band that we have never heard of, and would certainly not have made the effort to seek out.

The popularity of live music in pubs is largely due to the informal atmosphere in which the music can be enjoyed. We have not necessarily come, or paid, specifically to hear the band, as we would at a formal concert venue. This means that we can give as much or as little attention to the performers as we choose. We can sing along, humming through the bits we can't remember, without any embarrassment. If we get bored, we can leave, or move to another part of pub, without causing any offence.

We are also, both literally and psychologically, closer to the musicians in a pub than we would be in a concert hall or other music venue. The 'stage' may be no more than a slightly raised platform, and in many cases will simply be a corner of the pub from which the chairs and tables have been removed. There are no physical or psychological 'barriers' between the performers and their audience. This proximity increases both our sense of excitement at being 'part of the action', and the feeling of familiarity and friendliness. In other words, the novelty/familiarity factors which attract us to the pub in the first place are heightened by the presence of a live band.

Many pubgoers will boast that they 'knew' a now world-famous singer 'when he first started out playing in pubs'. They may never have spoken to the celebrity in question, but this does not mean they are exaggerating the friendship. There is a genuine feeling of intimacy between pub musicians and customers. Requests are called out, jokes and banter are exchanged, beers are offered and wrong notes are forgiven. In fact, any mistakes, broken strings or malfunctioning equipment will merely increase the sense of equality and good-natured tolerance between performers and audience. The musicians do not complain when we ignore them, or spill our beer on their 'stage'; we, in turn, do not expect polished perfection from our entertainers.

The informal setting and friendly atmosphere allows both performers and audience to relax and enjoy themselves.

Musicians appreciate these factors as much as we do. They welcome the opportunity to develop their skills and try out new ideas in an informal, sociable context. Many of the most famous performers began their careers in pubs, and pubs continue to serve as the training-ground for new talent. The unknown band playing in your local tonight could be hitting the headlines with their world tour next year. And even if you spend the evening chatting, drinking and paying little attention to the performance, you will be able to say "I knew them when..."

Do it yourself

In the old days, all of the music in pubs was 'live', and most of the musical entertainment was provided by the customers themselves.

Even the supposedly modern Karaoke merely gives structure to the old pub tradition of informal, spontaneous performances.

While the particular phenomenon of Karaoke may be a passing craze, we can be absolutely certain that it will soon be replaced by some other form of 'DIY' musical entertainment. Our need to perform, to show off and to laugh at each other will always be fulfilled, and this will ensure the survival of spontaneous, informal performances in pubs.

But how can we be so confident in our predictions? What makes this tradition so enduring? Why do we choose to indulge our exhibitionist tendencies in pubs?

The answer, again, lies in the unique combination of freedom and security that we experience in the pub. It is a place where we feel a little bit 'larger than life'. But it is also a place where we feel 'at home'. The excitement gives us the urge to perform, and the sense of security gives us the confidence to do so.

In the pub, we become less inhibited in our behaviour. We lose something of our natural reserve and we can get up and burst into

Karaoke is essentially a high-tech version of the traditional piano in the corner, where a regular or member of staff would sit and accompany any other customers who wished to display their singing talents.

song without embarrassment. A pint or two may help us to shed our inhibitions, but the context and atmosphere are far more important. Most of us would never dream of indulging in a solo performance on a train, however many gins we had imbibed in the buffet car. But in our local pub, even on orange juice, we will readily display our talent, or lack of it, for the entertainment of our fellow pubgoers. They may howl in mock agony if we sing out of tune, but they won't stand up and walk out on us. If we forget the words, our friendly audience will chime in. With a little help, we get by.

Background music

Much of the music we hear in pubs will not be 'live'. The background music, whether it is provided by a jukebox, tapes or a disc jockey, can be equally important. The licensee's choice of background music will have a significant influence on the atmosphere of the pub. The type of music, and the volume at which it is played, may determine both the type of clientele that will be attracted to the pub, and their behaviour while they are in the pub.

Publicans are well aware of this, and will select the music that the majority of their customers want to hear. For this reason, volumes and styles may vary according to the time of day. In a pub which attracts a 'business' clientele in the 30-40 age-group for after-work drinks, with a younger 'student' trade later in the evening, the barman will adjust the music to suit his customers' tastes. From 5pm to 7pm, he may play sixties and seventies tracks, which remind his customers of their carefree youth. At 7 pm, or whenever the younger element begin

Older managers and landlords may wisely leave the choice of music to bar staff of the same age-group and background as their customers, rather than attempting to keep up with the latest trends themselves. Such publicans may often be surprised, and highly amused, by a sudden craze for music of their own youth: a demand for 50s Rock & Roll, for example, or other 'retro' cults.

to predominate, the volume will be turned up, and the music will switch to the latest chart or 'cult' sounds. If any of the older clientele remain, this is their 'cue' to make room for the currently carefree.

The age of the main clientele is clearly the most influential factor determining the style and volume of the music in any pub. The novelty-seeking 18-25 age-group is perhaps the most demanding. The managers and staff of circuit pubs, theme pubs, fun pubs, disco-bars and student pubs have to keep up to date with the constantly changing cults and passing fancies of their young clientele.

The background music in pubs catering for an older clientele will vary according to the style of pub and the social class or background of the customers. In general, the higher up the social scale, the less up-to-date the music. The average 'stockbroker' pub, for example, will provide a steady diet of Roberta Flack and other soothing, 'timeless' female vocalists. In a council-estate community pub, catering to roughly the same age-group, the music will be more 'Radio 1' than 'Radio 2'. The exception to this rule is the 'yuppie' pub or up-market cafe bar, where the clientele may be over 30, and on the higher rungs of the social ladder, but like to feel they are touch with the latest trends.

Where there is a jukebox, the immediate selection will be determined by the customers themselves, but the publican still makes the initial choice of the type of music available. In many Irish pubs, for example, the jukebox will only offer Irish music. The publican and bar staff also retain control over the volume. This will usually be loud enough so that we know our selection is being played, but not so loud as to irritate those with different tastes.

There are also many pubs which have no music at all. These are often Serious-traditional pubs, or other self-consciously 'old-fashioned' establishments. The lack of music is always a deliberate policy, based on customers' wishes - or the wishes of the type of clientele that the publican seeks to attract. Some pubs may even proudly advertise the fact they that do not have music, usually naming several other features or facilities which they do not possess. The sign or advertisement will read "No Jukebox! No Pool Tables! No Fruit Machines!". It may seem odd to trumpet the absence of features in this way, rather than telling us what the pub *does* have to offer. But such advertisements do seem to have the desired effect. They attract customers who see the absence of music and games as a hallmark of traditional values, of a real, old-fashioned pub.

In fact, this is a somewhat misplaced nostalgia, as music and games are some of the most genuinely traditional features of pub life. But this does not matter. The customer is always right, and, as we have said before, the publican's aim is to please, not to give us a history lesson. Whatever our tastes, from heavy metal to peace and quiet, there will be a choice of pubs to match.

CHAPTER 5

More than a game

Like pub music, pub games and sports provide opportunities for the kind of interaction that facilitates social bonding. The British people are naturally somewhat reserved. We do not readily engage in conversation with strangers, and we lack the spontaneous warmth that characterises other less inhibited cultures. We need a good reason, a valid excuse, to initiate new relationships.

The pub itself provides the secure, sociable atmosphere which encourages friendly interaction. Pub games and sports provide the more immediate 'excuse' for initiating such interaction. Even if we are feeling in need of company, we are unlikely to approach a stranger who is sitting at a table with his pint, or with his mates. But if they are playing pool, bar billiards or darts, introductions become much less daunting.

Etiquette

Our natural diffidence, our reluctance to intrude on other people, means that we are always more comfortable when there are established 'rules of introduction' to follow. Knowing the 'etiquette', the correct form of address, gives us the courage to take the initiative.

For pool players, this is very straightforward. All you have to do is to approach a player and ask "Is it winner stays on?" This traditional opening is both an enquiry about the local rules on turn-taking, which may vary from pub to pub, and an invitation to play the winner of the current game.

The reply may be "Yeah, coins down" or "That's right, name on the board". This is both an

You may also make appropriate comments on the game - although it is advisable to avoid derogatory remarks. If someone makes a particularly good shot, the correct expression of approval is simply to say "Shot", although in this context the word is pronounced in a drawn-out manner, as though it had at least two syllables: "Sho-ot"

acceptance of your invitation, and an instruction on the pub's system for securing the table - which may be by placing your coins on the corner of the table, or writing your name on a nearby chalk-board. In either case, it is understood that you will pay for the game.

If the reply is simply "Yes", you may ask "Is it coins down?" or "Is it names on the board?". Having completed the correct introductions, you may now stand around, watch the game and join in the banter while you wait for your turn. Further enquiries about local rules are equally acceptable. These usually begin with "Is it", as in "Is it two shots on the black?" and "Is it stick pocket or any pocket?"

Every traditional pub game, from darts to dominoes, cards to cribbage, has its own etiquette, and its own 'coded' language. The uninitiated need to discover the rules, not only of the game itself, but of the associated behaviour and conversational style. This is not difficult. If we sit in the pub for a few evenings, watching and listening, we soon pick it up. And playing detective (or anthropologist) is an amusing way to pass the time.

The meaning of a 'coded' question, for example, may be revealed by the answer. An unfamiliar expression or gesture may be interpreted by observing exactly when it is used. If it always occurs after a successful shot, move, play etc., then it probably signifies approval or congratulation. Simply by watching, we learn the unspoken rules of behaviour: when to keep quiet, when to call out encouragement, whether the loser is expected to buy a drink for the winner and so on.

Becoming a warrior

If you become a regular in the pub, and show any aptitude for a particular game, you may be invited to play on the pub team.

If the presence of pub games provides opportunities for initiating

Many publicans place considerable trust in their 'warriors', and some team members may act as unofficial 'deputies' to the landlord. They may be relied on to ensure that everyone follows the rules, to prevent disputes and to protect the equipment from damage or misuse.

and developing new relationships, the pub team is the most effective means of 'consolidating' such friendships - reinforcing the social bonds within the pub. As a member of the team, you are no longer just playing darts, pool or dominoes for fun. You are playing for *your* pub, *your* 'tribe'.

The heightened sense of loyalty and 'belonging' among pub team members is evident in their manner and language. The word "we", for example, refers to both the team and the pub itself. ("Who are we playing in the first round?" "The Rose and Crown, I think.") This may seem trivial, but sports commentators who refer to Britain as "we" during international matches have been criticised for their lack of objectivity. And remember the patriotic outrage during the Falklands war when newsreaders were obliged to say "British troops" rather than "We" or "Our troops"? The easiest way to endear yourself to a new boss is to refer to your new company as "we" on your first day in the job. This is because the use of the word "we" to refer to a company, a nation or a pub is the most obvious indicator of loyalty.

Although the standard of playing may be high, and the competition fierce, the social functions of the pub team - the 'bonding' between members and the sense of 'citizenship' of the pub that is created - are equally important.

Joining the pub team is thus an important 'rite of passage'. All regulars feel part of the pub 'tribe', and many may treat it as a second home. But as a darts, pool, football or quiz team member, you become a 'tribal warrior'. You will go forth into battle for your pub, and return, in triumph or defeat, to cheers or sympathy - and sandwiches.

But your new status involves additional responsibilities as well as extra privileges. You will have noticed the 'proprietorial' manner of many established team members, their role as self-appointed 'guardians' of the pool table or darts board. These 'warriors' see the pub as their territory, and although they have no official authority, they do have a strong sense of responsibility for this territory. They will defend and protect their pub, as well as going out to battle against rival 'tribes'.

If the team members are young, you may find that the 'tribal elders' - long-standing, established regulars - will act as both supporters and supervisors of the young warriors. These 'elders' will be indulgent towards their charges, but will also check any excesses in their behaviour and help to ensure that they do not become over-zealous in their defence of their territory.

Ritual warfare

Playing against other pub teams in a local, regional or national league gives team members the opportunity to visit other pubs and test their skills against other players. Again, however, the social aspects of league matches are often more important than the competition. As one publican put it "I think our dominoes team are not so much interested in the game itself, but the opportunity to go to a different pub but still be with people they know."

League matches are clearly crucial to the formation and consolidation of 'tribal' bonds and loyalties. Groups are defined as cohesive social units in contrast to other groups. We have already noted the use of "we" and "us" to refer to both the team and the pub itself: to have a socially significant "us", we must also have a "them". The existence of a common 'enemy' or 'enemies' provides an external 'focus' for aggression, increasing the sense of solidarity within the group. In wartime, there is always a substantial reduction in violent crime and assaults within the countries involved in the conflict. The rivalry between pub darts teams may seem inconsequential in comparison, but it serves the same purpose - conflicts and

Like all ritual gifts, the post-match refreshments are not 'free': there is, as with round-buying, the expectation of a return. The 'host' team will expect to be offered food when they play at their rivals' pub. Equality is important in such ritual exchanges, and the host team will expect the refreshments at their 'away' matches to be of the same standard as those offered in 'their' pub.

tensions within the group are forgotten, as the members of the team are 'united' against their opponents.

League matches, however competitive, tend to be very sociable occasions. The 'hospitality rituals' associated with the matches help to promote friendly interaction between rival teams. These rituals will follow the usual 'unwritten' rules of hospitality and gift-giving.

At the end of the match, for example, the 'host' publican will usually serve sandwiches, soup and bread, hotpot or some other light meal to both teams. If the food is served from a counter, it is expected that the 'home' team will pass the dishes around to the opposing team, ensuring that all their rivals are served before they take their own plates to the table. Offering food to guests, and serving them first, is a universal gesture which, in all cultures, conveys a powerful 'message' of friendly and peaceful intentions. By accepting the gift of food, and 'breaking bread' with our rivals, we are effectively signing a 'non-aggression' pact. In this way, the traditional post-match hospitality serves to counteract any tensions or hostility generated by the competition.

From the 'host' publican's point of view, the meal is a 'thank-you' to both teams for the considerable extra custom which a match brings to his pub. Matches are usually played on otherwise 'quiet' weekday evenings, when the publican would not normally expect to do much business.

The manufacturers and retailers of games equipment, who constantly introduce new pub games into the market, are well aware of the importance of league matches. However high-tech or outlandish their products - from robotic boxing to bar flying -

THE CROWN
EVERY FRIDAY

INTERACTIVE BUNGY
JUMPING TABLE
FOOTBALL WITH
INFLATABLE
SUMO WRESTLING
QUIZ

£1· PER GAME

very few new games are introduced without the formation of at least a local league. The companies producing the games may even offer prizes to the winning team. There are now pub teams competing in inflatable sumo wrestling, interactive video quiz games, bungee running, air hockey, table football and bouncy boxing, as well as the more traditional darts, pool, bar billiards, football, dominoes and skittles. While many of the 'novelty' games will undoubtedly prove to be passing fads, they have the same fundamental, enduring functions as the more established pub games. They provide a medium for initiating, developing and reinforcing social bonds within the pub 'tribe'.

CHAPTER 6

Stars and bars

All the pub's a stage...

We have looked briefly at the role of the publican as 'actor', but what about the actor as publican? A number of well-known actors and other celebrities have 'retired' to run a pub, or do so alongside their show-business careers. Many more romanticise, like the rest of us, about 'retiring to run a quiet country pub with log fires'. So what is the attraction? Do the skills acquired on stage and screen help or hinder them in their new role? Are they different from other publicans, or do all publicans have an 'exhibitionist' streak? What new insights into pub life can a celebrity publican provide?

Melvyn Hayes, a comedy actor best known for his portrayal of a drag-artist in the television series 'It ain't 'alf 'ot, Mum', now runs a pub in St Albans. When we interviewed him, the pub had only been open, under his management, for six weeks.

He feels that his training and experience as an actor is directly relevant to his new role. "I think from my experience as an actor that I understand people," he claims "It's feeling the temperature and the climate of a person as he comes through that door...You've got to get to know your customers. People do like it if you start to pour their drink when they walk through the door, because they feel that they're special. Each person should be treated as if they're the most important person in the pub. When I'm in the theatre, I play it to the dress circle, the balcony and everywhere. You treat everybody the same and the whole audience should be like one. Same in a pub."

The actor's comments are fascinating, not because he tells us anything we didn't already know, but precisely because he is saying nothing new. If we remove the references to the theatre, this is exactly how all good publicans describe their role. Ask any publican who runs a successful, friendly, sociable pub how this is achieved, and he or she will talk about 'reading' the atmosphere, getting to know the customers, making them feel special, treating everyone equally and so on.

Perhaps, we might argue, it is Mr Hayes' training as an actor that has allowed him to pick all of this up in just a few weeks. This may be so, but then there are many other new

publicans who adopt the same approach from day one, without the benefit of previous experience on the stage. They just seem to have an instinct for what is right.

A more interesting explanation, therefore, would be that successful actors and good publicans share a number of the same personal qualities and instincts. The best actors, and the best publicans, are able to appear natural and relaxed in front of an audience, to leave their own problems behind and become the characters we want to see. Both have the 'gift of the gab', a sense of timing, and a talent for keeping us entertained. Both are acute observers of body language and atmosphere - they 'read' their audience and adjust their performance to our moods.

But the only true test of either an actor or a publican is the response of the customers. How was Melvyn Hayes received as the new landlord of the White Hart Tap? A celebrity publican will inevitably attract a lot of curiosity and attention, not least from other publicans.

"On the first night," he says, "it was packed, and there were twelve - and I mean *twelve* - other publicans in here. One of them, big guy, kept on leaning over and pressing my hand down on the pump, saying 'Hold the pump down, that's the way to do

The experience of
celebrity publicans
is somehow
reassuring. It
shows that we
pubgoers are not
impressed by fame
and glory, but will
readily show our
appreciation of the
natural skill and
diplomacy of a
good publican.

it, you've got no idea what you're bloody well doing, hold it down, hold it down.' So I couldn't stand it any more so I said 'You come round and show me how to do it.' He came round the bar, slipped on a glass, fell flat on his back. And while he was lying there, I said 'Oh I see, that's how to do it'".

No doubt the actor's unlucky neighbour is now telling the same story in his pub, with similar wit and equally impeccable timing - although perhaps with a different punchline.

On the whole, it seems that pubgoers are an egalitarian lot. Once the novelty has worn off - and it wears off very quickly - the celebrity landlord is given no special treatment. Mr Hayes' regulars would not allow him to join his own pub's Darts team unless he paid his 'sub', and informed him that this would be £7, because he was, on the day of his arrival, already six weeks in arrears. They then refused to let him to play at all, on the grounds that he wasn't up to their standard.

The behaviour of this celebrity's regulars is remarkable, not because they were unusually harsh, but because they treated him as any regulars would treat any new landlord. Regulars will always 'try it on' a bit with a new licensee. We will wind him up a little, make jokes at his expense, and generally test him out. Like children with a new babysitter, we will insist, wide-eyed and innocent, that the previous licensee *always* allowed us to stay on 'after hours'. We want to see what the new 'guv'nor' is made of, how far we can go. This initiation rite, this 'trial by regulars', is an ordeal that all publicans, however experienced and, clearly, however famous, must endure when they take over a pub.

Once he had settled in, and had a chance to demonstrate his good intentions, Mr Hayes began to receive the compliments to which he is, no doubt, accustomed. "We come in here because you talk to us," said a customer who had deserted his 'local' in favour of Mr Hayes' pub, because of the friendly approach of the latter. A local 'villain', taking pity on the innocent new landlord, even gave him some friendly advice on crime prevention: "Melvyn," he said "I just heard you say on the phone that you're closing in a minute and going out for Sunday lunch. Now villains like me will hear that and we'll break in. What you should say is 'I'll call you back', then people like me won't hear it."

Celebrity pubgoers

While celebrity publicans remain very much 'on stage' in their new careers, celebrity pubgoers seem to appreciate the chance to relax and 'be themselves'. Famous pubgoers find that they are not given any special treatment in their local pub. While they may be stared at and asked for autographs everywhere else, at their local, they are just 'one of the regulars'.

The well-known ITN reporter and thriller writer Gerald Seymour, author of *Harry's Game,* finds this comforting. "I had been away for five months covering the Aden troubles in 1967," he recalls, "and I had been on the box most nights. On my first night back I went into my local and somebody just said 'Hello Gerry, have you been away?'. That's the wonderful thing about pubs: it cuts you right down to size. The poseur has no place in a pub because he will just have his legs cut off at the knees and I like that."

Celebrities may well be subjected to a certain amount of teasing and mockery from the regulars in their local. TV actors are compared, unfavourably, to the

Only the most arrogant or insecure celebrity could resist such easy-going familiarity. For many, the local pub is a haven of normality, where they can escape from the pressures of being 'on display' and be treated like ordinary people. Like the rest of us, they feel 'at home' in their pub.

glamorous characters they portray. Well-known academics are invariably nicknamed 'Doc'. And world champion javelin thrower Fatima Whitbread frequently has to explain to the lads in the pub darts team that darts is not a miniaturised version of javelin throwing.

But then no-one is exempt from such banter. All regulars, however obscure, are given nicknames, or teased about some minor personal peculiarity. In the pub, a supporter of Manchester United will be the butt of just as many jokes about the team's fortunes as their star player. By mocking their local celebrity, the pub regulars are not giving 'special treatment', but quite the opposite.

Colin Dexter, world-famous crime writer and creator of Inspector Morse, took us for a lunchtime pint in his Oxford local. As we entered the pub, other regulars called out casual greetings, and by the time we reached the bar, Colin's pint of bitter and packet of peanuts were waiting. After a friendly chat with the publican, another regular approached. "I owe you a pint for that tip you gave me at the bookie's the other day," he said. Colin declined gracefully, pointing out that his friend's winnings on the Wales/England rugby match had later been lost on the horses.

Our visit took place in a week when Inspector Morse was in all the newspapers, and Colin was besieged at home by journalists trying to find out the Christian name of the enigmatic beer-swilling policeman. Yet in the pub, Morse was not mentioned once. Colin was able to relax and to give us his thoughts on the meaning and function of pubs.

"The pub is a separate circle of existence," he explained "You have your job, your family, circles that intertwine and overlap, but the pub is somehow outside that. It's another little world - like going to another country, but not very far away. It's a different ambience, a sense of independence, and that sort of feeling is very valuable. Above all, for me, it is the magic combination of friendship, conversation and beer - that form together a sort of alchemy of a very enjoyable piece of existence."

Celebrities, like the rest of us, need a 'circle of existence' which is somehow separate from our normal daily lives and troubles. We all need an independent sphere in which to enjoy, without obligation or constraint, the 'alchemy' of friendship, beer and conversation - the magic of pubs.

PUBS AND PUBWATCHING

Our aim in Pubwatching has not been to exhibit the unusual or extraordinary, but to convey something of the variety, complexity and 'magic' of ordinary pub life.

This kind of research is not, and should not be, an exact science. An account of pubs and pubgoing which contained only 'provable' facts and figures might be entirely accurate, but it could only provide a very narrow - and undoubtedly very boring - representation of pub life.

We leave such tasks to the market-researchers, who, with their clipboards and questionnaires, are better qualified to inform us on the precise percentage of socio-economic group C2/D who prefer lager to bitter, and other such important matters.

Our more 'fluid', anthropological approach - spending time in hundreds of pubs, observing, listening and talking with publicans and pubgoers - means that our conclusions are open to any number of queries and objections.

If any pubgoers wish to question our statements, or feel that they can provide more enlightening explanations, we would be happy to indulge in a 'Mine's better than yours' ritual, over a pint or two at the nearest pub.

We may not reach agreement, but we will derive greater enjoyment from our disagreement, and from each other's company, by arguing in the sociable atmosphere of the pub. There, the unspoken rules of pub discourse, and the bonds created by reciprocal round-buying, will ensure that our differences appear less and less important as the evening progresses.

We may even be distracted from our arguments by a live band, or a lively pub-quiz. Or we could be tempted away from our discussions by a game of pool or darts. If in doubt, we can always call on the guv'nor for arbitration. Most importantly, we can resolve our ritual dispute in the time-honoured, traditional manner: by pointing out that it is your round.

This is the 'special alchemy' of the pub, whereby the disinhibiting effects of beer are balanced by the gentle restraint of etiquette, a sense of freedom is combined with a reassuring familiarity and every ritual practice is designed to promote friendly interaction.

So, to the authors and readers of those doom-laden volumes with scare-mongering titles such as The Death of the English Pub, we can safely reply that rumours have been greatly exaggerated.

The pub, in all its manifestations, is quite clearly alive and well. And because it fulfils the fundamental human needs of social bonding, reciprocity, freedom and security, the pub will never die.